21st Century Psalms and Poetry

With Acronyms of Inspiration

21st Century Psalms and Poetry

With Acronyms of Inspiration

Tina S. Price

Ufomadu Consulting & Publishing

Published by:
Ufomadu Consulting & Publishing (UC&P)
P.O. Box 746
Selma, AL 36702-0746
www.UfomaduConsulting.com

ISBN 0-9754197-7-3
Library of Congress Catalog Card Number: 2005929192

Themes

LOVE

PSALMS

Preface

Acronyms are to the 21st Century what disco music was to the 1970's. A new era of exploration: As TIME passes people are using acronyms as a common part of their everyday language. The writings in 21st Century Psalms and Poetry challenge the mind to expand the horizon of acronyms in poetic expression and stimulates spiritual growth.

You will be pleasantly surprised HOW the poems interlink to other poems. When you find a poem with capitalized words within the text, use the table of contents to locate the word and read the poem. My HOPE is that you will find new meanings, insight and JOY within these pages and that you will PUSH yourself to continue to dream dreams, reach goals, and utilize your God given talents.

FEAR

Routine Religion

Oh, it is Sunday! Dawn of a new day!
Let's jump to get ready and go on our way,
Spruce up the dressing, polish the shoes.
Pack our dear pockets with "good tiding"
dues.
Turn that radio station to the gospel beat.
For this is not the day of the "blues"
worldly cheat.
Song after song, we like them all.....
Look out for Moma with the straightening
comb!
Get off the phone you can see your company
later,
Let us this day celebrate our Creator.

Off to the car, it's time to go,
to the place we think is a designated show.
HOW serious do we take this ritual?
Perhaps it has become merely habitual.....
Oh, well let us go through this weekly
display,
After all isn't it enough to just appear
today?
The drive to church is material it seems;

*The Cadillac is shining just look at the
gleam.
Nails and hair all freshly done,
Ties matching, handkerchiefs and
cummerbunds.
Our disposition, the lone deciding factor
whether or not we will become an actor
in the service at the Lord's house,
make a joyful noise or shhh!, be quiet as a
mouse.*

*Our arrival as always on schedule
We missed Sunday School the residual;
of Christian Education to equip for spiritual
warfare:
Do we not care about the importance of
being there?
maybe next week we will be on TIME,
For right now let's go in and chime
as brass cymbals in the devotional
and the Holy Spirit that dwells among us
moves, flows, breathes and comforts the
dust?
how then can we possibly continue the
motion?
Stand up, sit down, walk around, the
devotional;*

Trance in the state of body and soul
not releasing "us" to let GOD control;
The path that HE has already charted

our lives to pursue and be directed.
God makes all things purposely
and gives us the decision to edify Him
relinquish our being on this physical realm
prepare our souls for the continuum.

(Whoops! Stop, let's go back to the poem or
story,
It's just that GOD should receive glory.)

Where were we? Oh, yes, sitting on the pew.
The persona we possess is a stiff dark hue.
Who should bow in humble prayer?
Or smile, lift hands to praise, and worship
there?
Have we been programmed that church is a
solemn place?
And Sunday after Sunday just sit in the
space?
Here week after week to have a ball.
Looks like it's time for alter call.

Listen did he say the doors of the church are
open?
Someone jokes close them before SIN enters
in.
OH!!!!, Join the church and be a member?
But first review the duties we need to
remember;
What stipulations, not too much work and
should I witness?
Because this is no one else's business.
Benediction is here we made it through the
day
of Routine Religion now we are on our way:
To return to what we deem as living life
Monday to Saturday the physical/spiritual
strife.

FEAR
False Evidence Appearing Real

hat is the thing I FEAR the most?
Attacks against my tangible flesh?
Physical battle, hostility, blows from evil
foes?
Abuse, riots, poverty? All a hoax.
Things labeled FEAR frankly wear the seal
of False Evidence Appearing Real.

Which is to FEAR, man harming the flesh?
or GOD holding the proverbial soul loaned
to dust?

False is a lie that will never stand.
Evidence is proof to sway the opinion of
man.
Appearing is seen through the fleshly eye.
Real is the tangible senses that need to die.

GOD, our creator designed our SOULs
not instilling the spirit of this FEAR.
Wisdom, knowledge, discerning and power
He freely gave to us and showered

blessings to stand on the pillar of truth;
So, pulling the teeth of FEAR we shouldn't
loathe.

The victory won, the Lord is my light, my
salvation;
FAITH the key now and at creation.
Transposing the soul's intangible desire
to a new meaning of FEAR to take you
higher;
Face Everything And Respond in the light,
As a Christian Warrior propounding the
might,
of God's Word and Power which releases
the fear
of False Evidence Appearing Real.

SIN

Self Inflicted Nonsense

*The senses are the gateway in
the heart's desire and spectrum of **SIN**.
Touch, taste, hear, smell, and see
the fruit of remains shown forth from me
by selfish things that are and be;
Pride of life, lust of the eyes
these arrogances thrive my selfish desires.
I do it all unto the self
reaping havoc on a deteriorating health.*

*Stop **I**t Now! Things done by and unto self,
they ROB potential of life's great wealth;
HOPE came to give an abundant life
over pain, hatred, FEAR, jealously and
strife.
Stop **I**t Now! That self inflicted nonsense;
time and Time and TIME again,
release wicked desires that linger within
the senses that cause the deadly **SIN**.
Septuagint In Need, I AM To Be
covered by Jesus eternally!
Still In Need, I AM To Be*

His first fruit, my self, the me
through death's delivery process,
presented standing faultless
before God
despite SIN, that Self Inflicted Nonsense.

(The word Septuagint is a Hebrew word meaning: He keep watch over
my sins / Or has set a time for me / when He will)

FOOL

Full Of Our Lust

*The FOOL says in his heart,
there is no God.
His actions in life are callous and hard.
Letting the outside world enter in
a numb heart harboring lust and sin.
Then the flesh makes known
the types of seed the FOOL has sown;
Works of the flesh are made manifest
by hatred, adultery, wrath , uncleanness,
idolatry, witchcraft, lasciviousness
fornication, strife, and variances,
emulations, seditions, and heresies,
envy, murder, and drunkenness.
I tell you now none of which
shall inherit the kingdom by doing such
dark abominable idolatries called lust.
Causing the Temptor to gain a strong hold
for temptation to enter into the soul.
Full Of Our Lust; the Father is not
partaker of them who act as no cost,
has been offered up for the lost.
The works of the flesh are many indeed*

quite simply put it is lust, a seed
that shows in the one who lacks
wisdom, understanding, and sense of
knowledge
that God is the ultimate doctorate of life's
college.
Walk circumspectly, not as a FOOL
Welcome the Holy Spirit to reign in your life
and rule.

BAD

Beyond Artificial Divisions

What's so BAD about you and me?
Pride of life, lust of the eyes
mask our character
thru arrogance which thrives,
on hatred, FEAR, and selfish desires.
SOUL's are designed by God, our Creator,
and destined to receive HOPE by the
Mediator.

What's so BAD about you and me?
Thoughts we hold keep each other in
captivity.
You judge me by the complexion of my
sinew,
I judge you by the things you do.
Content of character, we dare not weigh
the who of a man in this day.
SOUL's don't have races, sexes, or
religions.
These things are merely artificial divisions;

What's so BAD about you and me?

We base importance on material wealth
Things do not make and keep our health.
All that we are and have is dust,
Clothes, cars, houses and us;
These stimulants are greed,
artificial wants and needs.
SOUL's don't have possessions
just housing in earthen mansions.

Truly our differences are not what they seem;
God arrayed us as flowers and so deemed
to carry life's mission;
Beyond Artificial Divisions.

BLAME

Be-Littling Are My Excuses

Spiritually starved and stone hearted is (s)he
whose contemptuous mind always BLAME
me;
Through excuses they BLAME to take focus
off self
casting aspersions on someone else.
The BLAMErs' desire is to oppress
and to produce an effect of fault and stress.
Truly this tool is a derivative of FEAR
to belittle, vilify, defame, and sear.
Any rise to esteem integrity and truth
are belittled, ridiculed, scorned by the aloof:
Destructive natures use BLAME to
denigrate,
get power over, disparage, and ultimately
hate
the 'thing" that resides within another:
'That God given talent" of a sister or
brother.
Love, grace, and mercy God has given
equally
reflect this towards each other often and
wisely.

Be prepared to take the BLAME for things
not going right
then release it to God, walk by FAITH, not
by sight.

ROB
Released of Bondage

he inclinations of doubt, guilt and FEAR,
rob me not to draw near:
To the One who opened His arms for me
and died that day on Calvary.
His blood was spilled that I might be
Released Of Bondage eternally.
Who then should rob me of my JOY?
Workers of iniquity plot to destroy
the eternal existence my SOUL will receive,
upon submitting my life's path to His will to
achieve.
Thus being Released Of Bondage through
JOY instead
of stricken down shame; preventing the
raising of my head.
What situation then should rob me of trust?
God after all made Adam from dust,
then released His Son the only redeemer
set precedence over death and left the
believer;
The Comforter who ROB me to clear

the webs of confusion that encompasses so de.ar.
When was I ROB and tell how?
Belief, acknowledgement, and confession made known;
A spiritual walk that I seek to atone
my natural mind to His likeness and image.
Why being ROB is an important lineage?
Truth, Prosperity, Victory, and Power
As a descendent of these by the great I AM
Released Of Bondage to inherit them.

SCAR
Soul Cut Analysis Revealed

*There is a SCAR, I can not reach
shown by tears of pain and each
passing sigh, serves as a reminder,
that next time I will not be kinder;
And give my heart to a fantasy
of earthly love, not beneficial to me.*

*What is this SCAR that enters me?
Probing my being and oozing beneath
seams of essence, between my sinew,
charting the course on a timeless sea,
beginning so perfect then ending with me.
Its' development birthed in the Master's hand
closed in dark deeps where my SOUL just stands,
out of scent, out of sight, out of touch, out of
sound
Viewing and experiencing all that's around.*

*The pain of the world not free at all,
Soul cuts are revealed through pits and
falls;*

Virulent diseased, a plague mental illusion
Alone one thinks for their finest conclusion;
Drawn for self, forget the best
interest of heart, in this human test.

Analyze that which has made you quivered
From this scar of heart you must be
delivered:
Alas, Soul's cry, 'the Apothecary's touch!'
Only He offers the cure, remedy as such;
a surgical penetration, a humanlectomy;
Chasten emotions, making me see
My eyes, were removed from Him, the key.

Wait to develop, the TIME to come;
Travel life's line, the ends will meet.
Soul scarred, lay bare at the Master's feet
Restore, Rejuvenate, Rebuild, Repeat
Refresh, Renew, Revive, Complete.
The journey revealed at last
as a SCAR, a lesson of the past,
an experience to remember
that next time I'll be kinder;
And surrender my heart to Christ
for love, for HOPE, for JOY, for peace
can only be found in His sweet release.

Sister, Sister

Sister, Sister haven't you heard,
of your value and treasure?
How often have you been told
of being a queen beyond measure?
You are indeed an ornament to admire and
be adorned.
Question, why the hardened lines of envy,
hate and scorn?
Mistily spread the face of Mother
Creation...
Thus unstabalizing the balance in law and
nature,
Re-creating our own disastrous low moral
stature.
The first teacher can no longer see,
what she teaches is apathy.
Caught up in our own perturbation:
Neglecting our children;
Their MINDS, the formation
of religion, values, culture we place
stipulation on someone else to take our
space.

*We use to bring forth Doctors, Judges, and
Inventors…
Now being replaced by others who enter
A country accepting anything that be,
other than that what looks like me.*

*Sister, sister don't you know? We hold the
seed,
Cultivate it to grow, In God, in FAITH, in
knowledge, in Power
We block our blessings they will not shower
Upon jealousy, gossip, malignancy
immoral, sinful, indecency.*

*Sister, sister, can't you see?
There should be no dissention between you
and me.
We are alike in our outer appearances.
Cut through the layers you'll find the
differences
of pain overcome to be a stronger degree
of God's grace and power to work through
me.
For where pain rules and abides, it cancels
the quality
of living upon FAITH, righteousness, love,
and dignity.*

Brother, Brother

rother, brother how long must we wait?
Til the sleeping giants began to awake.
Out of a conscious spell that seem to dwell
in the eyes and minds of men.

Brother, brother you seem to forget,
the history that has been writ:
On Sandy banks of Jordan's shore,
the call of God at Shechem;
Remember whom delivered you
and brought you through
a non violent process, to inheritance
of a equal rights success?

Brother, brother why be ambiguous of God?
You minds are tainted by the evilness of lies.
Somberly whispering the tie that binds
the crab in the bucket syndrome.
The comfort zone of circling the bottom, the
pit.
No longer seeking to raise up out of it.
Choosing not to remember God of
yesterday, today, tomorrow

wanting to replace Him with Buddha,
Hindu, and Allah.
Mere men will perish as these.
Remember whom delivered you on
your knees?
For God I live! For God I die!
The only battle cry means to survive.
Became yours and you chose to forget
who lifted you out of the pit?

Brother, brother it is TIME to awake!
And be God's chosen vessels in a conscious
state.

POT
Prophet Of Tears

In the clay POT therein lies;
the profit of my countless tears.
It contains the bondage of many FEARs
built over the ages of vested years.

The suffering at times was
inflicted by those
whose hatred and jealousy arose
to prevent me, knock me, off my feet.
Rather revenge, I prayed and took the leap
of FAITH, giving thanks that things will all
work out;
for me the tears, sleepless nights and doubts
being contained in a vessel, a jar, clay POT;
someday to be used as an ensample to
others;
When suffering hits, you are overcomers.
Suffering? A SCAR, a test burning through
selfish desires to make the POT a new;
FAITHful vessel to be used in the kingdom
of God

Rather fight, surrender, releasing may be hard.

Become a servant as Mephibosheth
Be humble, patient, and meek knowing that
The table is set before those against you
To view grace, mercy, and bountiful
blessings too.
There's HOPE in suffering to produce a tool
vigilant of character, bravery that rules.
In spite of countless, cries over the years
none were in vain, they washed the FEARs;
And produced a FAITHful vessel, a Prophet
Of Tears.

One Step Between Me and Death

One fact about 'living' there is to know,

every man's life is a vain picture show.

Heaping up riches, goods and wealth

Not knowing the inheritor of things after

death.

Thinking we are in some type of control

neglecting the Sustainer and Maker of

SOUL.

Each breath we take we are in the midst

of God's spirit being in it;

for vapor and dust is all the body be,

and this is the step between death and thee.

Each action is weighed by the Creator

Himself.

Glory to God is why we were made

and the dead in the grave is silent and laid,

to rest.

So forget not, in this life we are in death.

God alone sustains all in all

*and when He summons our being we must
obey that call.*

'One Last Tuck'

The Father's fold of the satin sheet
done so smooth to make it look neat;
Looking down on that child of his,
wishing he was still a kid.
The dreams he had for this child,
could not be uttered yet for a while;
For now is the time to get the last look,
roll the cradle, close the book.
One last tuck and the Father stood,
back from the child as to watch
the deed he had done, so very much;
now in the hands of the undertakers' touch.
'One last tuck', the Father's soul cried
from birth to manhood all he tried
was to raise his child in the biblical way;
As stated by the preacher in the eulogy that
day.
Standing to see the earth opened up
to receive the final crib that cradles like a
cup.
'One last tuck' and the dirt was thrown
signaling the end, the Father had known
the one true thing that we all must get

upon entering the world and leaving it;
One Last Tuck
and the son entered quick
opened his eyes in the midst of it;
The morning of eternity, beautiful array
of glassy seas, misty singing breeze, dew so
sweet,
and angels at bronze feet.
The son went right in those arms of His
entered into rest, closed his eyes for the final
and best
tuck and fold was there at last:
Safe with the Father, Son, and Spirit.
'One last tuck', earthly father thanks so
much
your guidance to the Savior led me home,
now I am safe in divine Holy touch.

LOVE

Parousia!

(Meaning a 'royal or official visitation' from God)

ear God,
Why can't I control the love in my heart?
Make it began, make it depart?
'My child', He says, so carefully,
'through you I'm expressing divinity.
As SIN entered the world through Adam,
the one
My gift of LOVE was Jesus to bond
the pains, hurts, ills the world doth gives.
So, HOPE is here you won't be
disappointed,
Your choice in action of LOVE is anointed;
Parousia! It's Me! A visit that's counted,
destined in heaven and, on My throne it's
mounted.'
And tell me why I am to BLAME
for past selfish acts of people which aimed
arrows, darts of destruction that shattered
the human heart in separate parts?
'Remember this My precious one,
another child's hurt from the past should
see

the Christ in you reflected from Me.
My LOVE I give to flow is free
just do your part FAITH-fully.
I sealed your heart with My Holy Spirit,
of LOVE, JOY, peace, longsuffering, and
such
gentleness, goodness, FAITH, a bunch
of meekness and temperance to name a few
gifts;
sent from Me in heaven above.
Delivered in you earthen vessel through the
dove.'
And God, this hurts, I give my all
I feel rejected and in for a fall.
'Beloved, what you feel, still is of Me
I sacrificed My Son you see,
in order for gifts and all these feelings to
be.
Rejection, I know, I created it too
experienced it first hand, way before you.'
Well my Lord, I don't understand;
What do I give, without the plan?
'LOVE is all you're commanded to owe
in-spite the actions someone else might
show.
Persevere that too is your part;

I AM using My vessel who said from the heart,
"I accept You Jesus, and it's <u>Your</u> LOVE
I will give to those in my path You chose."
Yes, my Lord, I'll continue in your bond
and as the TIME of life goes on;
I will travel life's line, til the ends do meet.
Lay bare a SCARred SOUL at my Master's feet,
a charge I have to Him, to keep.
'Gird yourself, I AM here
to always protect, trust, hope, and persevere.'
Amen!

I AM

Indefinitely Always Me

The beginning;

To Be the way, truth, and life, I AM the

method, message, and meaning.

To Be the vine, I AM the sustainer of life.

To Be the Bread of Life, I AM the source for

eternal life.

To Be the light of the world, I AM the Word

of spiritual truth.

To Be the Good Shepherd, I AM love and

guidance.

To Be the gate for sheep, I AM the only way

into God's kingdom.

To Be the resurrection and life, I AM the

power over death.

To Be the Son of Man, I AM divinely human.

To Be your redeemer, I AM your sacrifice.

To Be on the right hand side of God's

throne, I AM your intercessor.

To Be an inheritor of the kingdom of God, I

AM,

To Be alive in you, I AM omnipotent,

omniscient, omnipresent,

I AM Indefinitely Always Me!

An eternal promise, To Be;
never ending.

LOVE

Life, Our Victorious End

The Prosecutor bargaining for a guilty
decree:
HOW much LOVE can someone give,
to a prideful person who intends to live
life their way at all cost?
HOW much LOVE will be lost
when conceit and arrogance is the thrust
in the gateway of eyes full of lust?
HOW much LOVE will be wasted
on a narcissism attitude that hasten
time as if it doesn't matter?
HOW much LOVE will be shattered
by a self-important ego
believing the lie that it is all about the I?

The Defense Attorney (DA) intercedes:
The walls of defense were broken down,
(Opening his hands to show his palms core)
but LOVE is God's truth and nothing more.
To create a life and then meet defeat
(Shaking his head while looking at his feet)

is a travesty offence against God's LOVE.
Water and blood was shed above all faults
(Touching His sides as proof)
to save sinners, the sick, the aloof.
All with my name will return thru me
(Smiling towards his Father, on bended
knee)
for I was there at LOVE's first start
and the Judge and I are one in heart.

The Judge's final response:
Putting Hate vs LOVE in prospective reality.
LOVE was created by My son and Me.
(With one swift nod to the DA on His right)
He has made his plea and the
verdict is easy.......
Not guilty.

FAITH

Forsake All, I'll Take Him

*1 God's revelation is His Son
the appointed heir of what's past, present
and to come.
*2 Jesus' total submission
let the Father's will be done.
*3 Moses the FAITHful servant but Christ the
Son
*4 Jesus the Great High Priest
made rest available to all
*5 by His obedience through suffering
made FAITH perfect in he,
the author of eternal salvation, navigator of
life's sea:
*6 Being steadfast in FAITH
to receive the unchangeable Oath;
Christ is the veil of our HOPE,
*7 the new order of Priesthood
consecrated so that He could
intercede for those that repent.
*8 Christ Ordained The New Covenant
*9 Jesus' Blood entered the Holiest Place

50

obtained eternal redemption for the human race.
[10]Christ's Sacrifice perfects mankind and the just living by FAITH are patiently sanctified.
[11]The Power of FAITH form that which is unseen without it; it is impossible to please the King.
[12]Jesus the author and finisher of FAITH makes the fruit of God's chastening easier to take.
[13]Love, praise, and thanks to He, our duties of chastity.
Sovereign glorified Lord of all to be; worshipped in fidelity
Obedience the seed in those who proclaim, Forsake All, I'll Take His name!

*The 13 Chapters of Hebrews

HOPE

Heaven's Operating Power Eternally

eaven's Operating Power Eternally,
the grace and mercy given to me
from God our Father thru unfailing LOVE;
Sent HOPE, Jesus, His Son from above.
All that I need to cover me
is in Heaven's Operating Power Eternally.
At times slayed, yet I have HOPE.
To comfort, convict, and compel me to cope,
to carry His commission and be a voice;
Echoing the FAITH of those He foreknew
would live towards the destined path to
inherit His kingdom, that justified few
wear the helmet of HOPE, of salvation
to remind the world of propitiation.
In His Word I place my HOPE
that
redemption is over, settled, I'm Free
by Heaven's Operating Power Eternally.
Sanctification by His Holy Spirit
thru TIME and endurance there remains to
be
the HOPE of glory to see Christ in me.

Behind the veil we have HOPE that our anchor
withstands the storm and sets the sail
towards the everlasting HOPE of eternal life;
Glorification, the ultimate state we will be
after Heaven's Operating Power Eternally
rests in the HOPE of eternal life
with God our Savior, Jesus Christ.

DNA Declaration
Divine Nature Attained

hereas,
*Only through the knowledge of God
grace and peace will multiply.
His divine power gives us all
things that pertain to life and godliness;
And be it furthermore since
He called us to glory and virtuousness:
Therefore giving great, precious promises
as partakers of divine nature which has
escaped from corruption in the world of lust.
And being resolved this, giving all diligence,
add to faith; virtue, knowledge, temperance,
patience, godliness, charity and kindness.
Whereas, if in you these things abound and be
they make you neither barren nor live
fruitlessly.
Be it resolved that:
He which lacks these things of truth be
blind, unseeing afar, and in SIN's captivity.
Therefore be it resolved,*

*give diligence to make sure your election
and call.
For with God's DNA, you shall never fall:
And Thru Christ's Witness Whereof,
an entrance shall be ministered abundantly
into the kingdom of eternity.*

JOY, I AM!

Just Over Yonder, I AM!

ust Over Yonder I AM and wait,
til My Spirit takes root in it's earthly state.
Parting the SOUL and dropping the seeds
of LOVE, peace, and joy it so desperately
needs:
Watering with HOPE, making things work
for the best
growth and development of daily tests.

Just Over Yonder, I AM in wonder,
of creatures given earthly dominion to
ponder;
And the selfish narcissistic tendency to be
above, separate, and exclusitivity.
Longsuffering, gentleness, goodness it takes;
blessed is the one who knows what's at
stake.

Just Over Yonder, I AM and watch,
the building of veils that cover the face,
shackling the minds of the human race.

Strong holds of FEAR, the conscious thrives
upon entering the world of illusion and lies;
The battle within each SOUL is to be free,
to express its' mission would break the
captivity.

Meekness, temperance, and FAITH the last
fruits,
nestled in JOY betrothed unto you
by the vine of life's foundation, forever
anew.

Just Over Yonder, I AM until
all that has departed from Me indwells
the knowing of My Spirit, LOVE, Peace, and
JOY;
willingly expressed by man, woman, girl and
boy,
The heavenly Jerusalem awaits your
entrance,
to kingdom's rest on the great shore
where, JOY, I AM forevermore.

This Day's Pardon

I AM pardoned and forgiven of me
are transgression, guilt, FEAR, and iniquity.
Acquitted by FAITH through HOPE to see
Jesus loosed my soul and set me free.
So, vindicated I AM and free from BLAME
the past is past, no need for shame.
Peace I have for I AM clear,
exempt, excused, exonerated,
never in life to be berated.
JOY I have accepted this gift
and start this day off with a lift
of prayer, praise and thankfulness
for God's unwavering LOVE and
FAITHfulness.
This day anew
with my promise remaining true;
Pardoned I AM,
released of the ordinance of death that be
the wage of SIN eternally.

WIT

Walk In Truth determined by the Way I Think

Charge can be challenging but here's what
to seek:
Strive to be like Christ, the great mercy seat.
Operate in fullness and the purpose thereof
by studying God's Word to know what's
above
the pains, hurts, and ills the world gives.
<u>Remember</u> <u>the</u> <u>promises</u> of God to give
abundant life.
Know in this world the subtractor is strife.
Walk In the Truth of the great I AM
God the Creator, Sustainer, Provider
Jesus the Savior, Intercessor, Redeemer
Holy Spirit the Comforter, Convictor, and
Compeller
Simultaneous triune, functions made one.
**So have WIT to know your enemy is
retreated;**
The flesh, the world, and Satan is defeated.

*(Christ's obedience to the cross made way
for none to be loss.)
The enemy functions are to ROB, kill, and
destroy
TIME, talents, and finances, so abhor
SIN, negativity, and lust.
Have WIT to know earthen vessels return to
ashes and dust.
The WIT then goes back to the Creator
breath of life given from the Sustainer;
Spiritual WIT adorned for Christ
to be accepted or rejected in His glory
will be the ultimate price.*

SOUL
Shadow Of Unending LOVE

Shadow Of Unending LOVE

descending from heaven like a dove,

fill me with aromatic sensations.

Live for now, avoid earthly destinations

of pain, deceit, fear, lonely solitude.

Enter the bliss thru nude,

openness, truth, character, courage

based on these there is no storage

of what was, what happened, what should be;

just a life to live, that is the key.

AOL

Author of Life

I AM the One, the Author of Life,
sitting on the throne with My Son who atoned
*the SINs of the **world**, then leaving on loan*
My Spirit to convict, comfort, and compel
My souls on earth to follow the path which
dwells
a fulfillment of life in humanistic form
til the RIP in the veil of the curtain is sewn.
Conductor of events, past, present, future
I take the rod, sword, and sutures;
Deleting old nature, downloading the new
primed, pruned vessel through and through.
Yes, I AM the One and Only True Source,
The AOL, that charters the course.
Setting the sail on the earthly sea
calm or troubled, whatever the case may be;
Surf with care, I will always be there.
*Arms open **wide**, enter into 'My Net',*
with safety, no disease, no virus to detect..
*One secure **web** site for all mankind,*
WWW.Divine

W.W.W.Divine

The prayers of the righteous availeth much,
they are totally in tune to God's touch.
W.atch, he instructs, and I will pour
you out blessings forevermore;
Stay in the path that is narrow,
the Word of God, Truth , shall be the arrow.

Now you have prayed, move your feet;
To step out on FAITH means not taking a
seat,
Rather W.onder in praise of His miraculous
power.
There's a hedge of protection around you
that towers,
over all harms, hurts, and dangers.
Remove thyself for God is and shall be.

What is left to be done? We might ask,
After prayer and praise it is TIME to bask!
W.ait on the Lord for all your answers.
Meditate, listen, and the Holy Spirit enters;
guiding us through our petty trails and
concerns.

63

Always an experience and lesson to be learned.
Building blocks of character and moral structure within,
our humanistic self that our SOUL is penned.

After standing and standing and standing some more,
God our Creator will open any door.
To Him be the glory that is the key,
He is the true source of the vine for mankind
Omnipotent, Omnipresent, Omniscient is He,
Upload WWW.DIVINE and you will see.

TIME

Things I Must Earn

hings I Must Earn are allotted to me
by a process based on a continuum;
Of growth, not just mere physically
based on time and life's momentous speed
But spiritually, mentally. and
psychologically.

Things I Must Earn are available in season;
not of my own but of God's due reason,
To provide the needs that I must have
And when I am able to be a wise steward
The TIME of wants will be established and
pleasin',
Thanks to the removal of me, myself, and I,
The fleshly creature sinks and die.

Things I Must Earn are taught through life,
Ironically embellished in pain, stricken
strife;
Victoriously removed on the other side of
through
Simply because TIME has defeated the coup.

Lessons of patience, really mean sit and be still
All things will work; God has a purpose and will.

Things i must earn are simply not free;
a husband, a wife takes TIME to be,
job promotion, new house, clothes, and car:
Materialistic matters will all pass,
God has TIME in the palm of His hands
Outstretched and open for your taking,
Walk right in, there will be no mistakin',
Identities of TIME distributed by the Creator
Solely for you and at His pleasure,
He died on the cross because you, He reassures.
Things I Must Earn equals TIME
The Father measures
the extent he grants you to complete your purpose
with cleaned iniquity
on this shore in the middle of His eternity.

S. O. S.

The Shelterer Of Spirit,
Master Carpenter bestowed
the S.O.S., Savior of Souls
who made available to disburse and appoint
unto those
the Spirit Of Solomon aroma of the Creator
official, anointed Jerusalem Temple maker
man of foundation, wise, from the Master's
touch,
carpenter, brick layer, overseer and such:
the pillar of strength, assured confident
patient, consistent, and obedient.
Spirit of Solomon builder with wood and
brick
the martar, clay, tools and elements
shall serve your command
to form the vision placed in your hand.
Now Spirit of Solomon, to you a charge:
Build the temples, that shall house
the new Jerusalem, the church, the spouse.
For the new Covenant came, the Son of
Sons, fulfilled the law
redeemed lost souls and left them that are

as traveling tabernacles and witnesses on earth.
A place they need to testify of His worth;
for their souls in dwell the ark covenant of His blood
and the praise of His people shall be heard.
Remember!
God's presence shall come to the temple you built
as Flowers array, Solomon of Spirit.

Father, I AM

Framed in a structure of strength and
might,
Essence of power and soul out of sight.
Father, I AM what you released me to be;
An example for the world to see!
Your teachings of temperance, worthy of
respect,
shine from sons and daughters, you did not
neglect;
Responsibilities of developing principles and
character,
Yet planning the TIME to prepare me
further
for my future inheritance of never ending
love.
Father, I AM what you made me from above.
Joy, peace patience, kindness and love,
Goodness, FAITHfulness, gentleness, self-
control
All learned from you earthly father who
hold;
Accountability for growth development of
the home,

Squarely on the shoulders of your frame.
Father, I AM and shall always be
a portion of you
throughout eternity.

Father, I Will

Sun up, sun down, I worked the fields
Reaping a harvest to eat fresh meals;
Ailing in health my taste buds are subtle,
No longer enjoying favorite feasts;
Whom then will enjoy the hot meals and
treats?
Sit in my chair and ease their feet,
while enjoying the smell of the kitchen's
savor, sweet ...

I heard a voice that vaguely squealed,
Father, Father, Father I will.

The house, no longer am I able to paint;
My hands are feeble, weak, and faint.
Please keep it up
and remember each stroke
was laminated with care and prayer
for them that dwelled and visited there.
And whom will cover my widow and
orphans now left alone?
Protect them from harm and dangers
unknown...

Father in spite of your hurts and ills,
Father tis' I, and Father I will.

My steps have slowed to a shuffling pace;
Not able any longer to run life's race.
My sight has dimmed.
Yet vision remains,
to guide me along this road that twines.
So, whom should take this walking stick,
to clear the path of weeds, vines in the
thicket?

The voice again, I hear so very clear;
"Father, Father, I surely will."

My senses have aged in this earthen vessel.
Yet I hear the call for me to nestle;
'Lie down, working one, lie down.
Rest In Peace you have a crown.'
As I'm escorted in, it's hard not to look
back;
For wondering whom will take the tasks,
perform the deeds I've done,
taking the reigns, and carrying on...

"Father the answer of course is still,
Father tis' I, and Father I will."

(This poem written in memory of my Father, William Hardy Smiley,
Sr., and to my Brothers, William, Johnny, and Arthur)

PUSH! PUSH! PUSH!

Pray Until Something Happens

The walk I took I thought I controlled,
every aspect of the way.
Until I fell and landed in a desolate world
one day;
No family to reach, no friends to call,
The mirror to face was all
I felt was left to PUSH the agony away.
The reflective image of me;
Pierced my eyes to see
I could not run from what's above
So, on my knees I prayed.
'Dear God of all, it's me again
now humbled before your throne.
Have mercy on my SINful SOUL
And grant me peace from now on.
I know you did not intend for me
to harbor greed, hate, and strife.
Your divine will and purpose I want
to manifest in my life.
I believe in Jesus Christ, your son
you sent to pay the price,

that cleansed me from all unrighteousness,
now use me as a witness.
Create in me a clean heart
And dwell there through, and through...
Amen'
Now done praying a sinner's plea;
The conceptual thought of being free
gestates the inner being.

HOW

Have Open Will

HOW to forgive those who hurt?
Their jealousy and envy, lies in lurk
to ROB my JOY, my LOVE, my peace.
The pain weighs more than the eye can see.

HOW to withstand the pressures of life?
Thoughts of FEAR cut like a knife.
HOW to cope
with life's ups and downs?
Money being tight, no resources 'round.

HOW do I do this? Please, let me know!
The path of the world, so BAD and frowned;
Mankind eventually lets you down.
I searched the earth, to find the solution
was there all the TIME, amidst the pollution.

Have Open Will the battle's not yours,
One man birthed SIN into earth's doors.
Righteousness, justice, would all be a lie,
if convicted for Adam's mistake, then die.

Have Open Will you're not made to FEAR,
He holds you close to His heart so dear.
Like His Son, the HOPE of mankind,
upload WWW.Divine.
Have Open Will to what comes your way,
and just do your part, day by day.

PSALMS

Righteous Love

There are those who claim love has no
boundaries.
It raises with the beautiful Pleiades...
It sets beneath the deep earth's door,
No depths to reach, no heights to soar...
Just sweet sentimental longing that reach
the inner core.
As was such, the moment of touch
the fulfillment of my need.
To whisper words of descriptiveness
is hush utterance of the seed,
That began to grow some years ago
by passing chance indeed...
Our paths crossed in love's abiding loss.
The Catalyst shall not be
for I alone reach for the door,
wondering will you stop me?
No, not a thought or expression,
Do you surmise the connection?
Even then so after placing HIM last,
The bide for me He cherished:
Discovering this one lonely night,
while weeping well til dawn
His voice breezed through a prism dew

"The best is yet to come!"
In succor anticipation for me alone
His boldness was profound:
He caressed me, He stroked me, He singled
me out
not caring who was around.
Attractive the eyes of the one,
who reached inside thee hourglass.
He patiently waited for my time to pass,
inquisitively counted each particle of sand
and held the glass pieces in His hand.
Knowing, how fragile I must be
He remolded, reshaped and defragmentized
me.
His graceful giving is all my living
was mapped out to be.
For HIM alone I return myself
as a living sanctimony.
I deserve nothing, who am I to think
that I control my sinew?
It is He who allows me to work His vineyard
thru.

Timeless on earth the whisper
of essence He controls it all.
I love HIM so, I will not let go
JEHOVAH-TSIDKENU

PSALM 84:11

I AM a sun on the river of life
a bask of JOY in sorrow and strife,
Waiting my child to fold and tuck
your troubles away beneath the dock.
I AM the shield, a great protector
blocking arrows, blows, and a deflector.
Giver of grace, glory, and mercy
unmerited favor and goodness to the thirsty;
Blessed are those whose walk is upright,
and are seeking the Savior day and night.

Our First Dance

Our first dance, I shall never forget!
You were not there to hold me and yet
soft crescendos of LOVE resounded in the air
with the essence of You everywhere.
I moved on the floor thinking of You
allowing my senses to experience the new
completeness You bring
then my heart began to sing.
And within me my desire above any thing
is for our LOVE to remain and ring
the Spiritual dance of LOVE.

PMS
Praising My Savior

This shall be written for generations to come
wonderfully made daughters and sons;
Worship, commend, admire, glorify
the One who came down to nullify,
the wage of sin; death penalty it was to be.
But mercy came through Jesus for you and
me
So offer to God
a sacrifice of praise continually.
Yes, temptation and trials come each day
But His Word is true, hold fast anyway.
The fruit from lips that confess his name;
<u>Must</u> put on a garment of praise and be
ordained:
Anointed to preach, to teach, to heal
every yoke of bondage that rob, kill, and
steal.
In His presence is fullness of JOY;
and at his right hand are pleasures for
evermore.

The Dance of Love

Welcome me with your eyes my sweet;
fiery the rhythm upon our meet.

Your touch, a rush to my heartbeat
it begins to take a soft cha-cha leap.

Aroma of you do fill the air,
inhale your scent is all I care
to do from now til my timing ends;
and the life of music my SOUL rescinds.

Taste of your kisses, my favorite dessert;
Spin me in a frenzy of love that work
the sound of sighs expressed from the deep
essence of me which oozes beneath,
that which makes me quickly release.

Treble, I am, while under your touch;
Soft crescendos of love and much
care and concern spring of each pore,
knowing you'll be there forever more.

A Candle

Brilliance of life!

Resonating through strife!

I shine a clear way so all may see

That Jesus is LOVE and

That He resides in me.

Abiding peace in hearts,

Not yielding to FEAR

Yearning, burning, JOY forever warm and

near.

(An acrostic for BRITTANY)

Psalm of My Be-LOVEd

Thou are fair my LOVE,
beholding me with the eyes of a dove;
full of LOVE, grace, and mercy
Turn away thine eyes,
for You have overcome me:
My beloved is mine and I AM His:
I sit down under His shadow with great
delight.
His fruit is sweet to my taste and sight.
Thy lips, o my Spouse, has the honeycomb
drip:
under thy tongue is honey and milk.
I AM my beloved and He is mine.
He takes me to the banqueting house of
Zion,
and His banner over me is LOVE.
Thou art in the clefts of the rock, my dove,
dwelling in the secret places of the stairs:
Let me see thy countenance, I stare.
Let me hear thy sweet voice;
For you are my choice.
Beautiful countenance in whom

there is no spot.
I AM my beloved's and his desire is towards
me.
His left hand is under my head,
and His right hand embraces me.
The roof of His mouth is like the best wine
from my beloved,
that goeth down sweetly, causing my lips to
speak:
'My beloved is mine, and I AM His.'
Many waters cannot quench LOVE, neither
can the floods drown:
if a man would give all the substance of his
house for LOVE,
it would utterly be condemned and fall to the
ground.
For true LOVE isn't contained nor
measured at all.

Humanistic Self

You!
Mesmerize with a twinkle in your eye each
TIME
electrical shock waves shimmer up my
spine;
defying unspoken laws of human
imagination,
breaking barriers of matter and space
amalgamation.
Increasing the blood flow in my heart's
pump...
You!
Set in motion, a powerful stillness that
drives
deliverance of LOVE, which thrives
on freedom from such
divine devotion of your touch...
You!
A source of grace undisguised;
mask my flaws with patience until I
seize the moment of human existence
and run this race without resistance.
You!

*Serve my Humanistic Self with mercy and
LOVE
totally, thoroughly, completely, above
the pressures of life, mankind's agenda,
blocking the path of those seeking to
'hinda';
the experience of my Humanistic Self...
You!
Each TIME you look my way, light the fire
of life
within my Humanistic Self and I know
I AM alive!*

POP

Paean of Praise

ure! I shout, I sing, I wave,
letting the world know I am saved!
To what avail this character, this demeanor,
of exclaiming to the world, I have a
Redeemer?
For if to show, I am just human dust
come to express my POP is just
an impression in the mirror of TIME to be
one with my Savior in eternity.

Sure! I cry, I laugh out loud,
At times alone and amidst the crowd.
For can mere man dictate to me
how Glory, Grace, and Mercy be?
Not at all for his thoughts are like mine
raveled, twisted, torn, and twined.
But HOPE is there in the midst of my POP
changing my heart, changing my thought.

Sure! Paean of Praise
on this earth is a phase;
a rehearsal that mirrors my FAITH, my
JOY,
my love, my peace;
Placed by God on earth, on lease.
Til His call, the one that is to summon
His angel to me, to tell me to comin'
To rest, to love, to shout, non stop;
A Heavenly Host of Angels, me, and the lot
going down 'The Soul Train Line' just doing
'the POP'!

LOVE's End

My mind
allows
the thought
of Your being
to encase me.
Willingly
my emotions
become dull
of past hurts.
Hoping
You to be
the final chapter
of LOVE.

Acknowledgements

Special thanks and recognition to:

God, in all that I am may your glory be seen to praise.

Christ, the savior, redeemer, and intercessor forever.

The Holy Spirit, for being here to comfort, convict, and compel me to go up a little higher.

My birth parents:

Mr. William H. and Mary B. Smiley

My surrogate parents:

Mr. James and Etta Perkins

My spiritual parents:

Dr. Frederick D. and Ailene C. Reese

Pastor Alan and Pam Yarbrough

Especially my precious children:

Timorra and Kirk (II) Price.

The people who touched my life, whether it was in a good, indifferent or any other type of way, You all made this book possible.

To order additional copies of:

21st Century Psalms and Poetry

With Acronyms of Inspiration

Call 334-418-0088
Or please visit our website at:
www.UfomaduConsulting.com

NOTES

NOTES

NOTES